PLANTS

By

William Anthony

BookLife
PUBLISHING

©2019
BookLife Publishing Ltd.
King's Lynn
Norfolk PE30 4LS

ISBN: 978-1-78637-560-5

Written by:
William Anthony

Edited by:
Holly Duhig

Designed by:
Gareth Liddington

CONTENTS

Words that look like <u>this</u> can be found in the glossary on page 24.

WHAT IS A PLANT?

Plants are living things that need different things to survive.

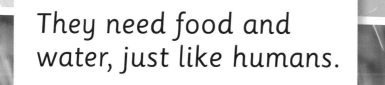

They need food and water, just like humans.

Water is very important for plants.

5

TyPes Of PLaNTs

Some plants you might see outside are flowers and trees.

FLoWErS

TRees

LOTUS

WATER
LILY

Some plants live in water,
such as water lilies and lotuses.

GROWING UP

Sunflowers are one of the tallest flowers.

Plants need food, water and sunshine to grow big and tall.

Did you know that plants can make their own food?

Plants use sunshine and air to make food.

ROOTS

ROOTS

A plant's roots are usually found underneath the soil.

Roots help the plant stand up. They also <u>absorb</u> water from the soil.

Roots are long and twisty, like string!

STEMS AND TRUNKS

The tall part of the plant is called the stem. It stands above the ground.

STEM

Trees have bigger stems called trunks.

TRUNK

The stem carries water from the roots to the rest of the plant.

LEAVES

Leaves grow from
the plant's stem.

There are many different types of leaves. Some are spiky and some are flat.

PINE NEEDLES

OAK LEAVES

FLOWERS AND FRUITS

Lots of plants grow flowers at the top of the stem.

Do you have a favourite flower?

APPLE TREE

Some plants grow flowers that turn into fruits, such as apples.

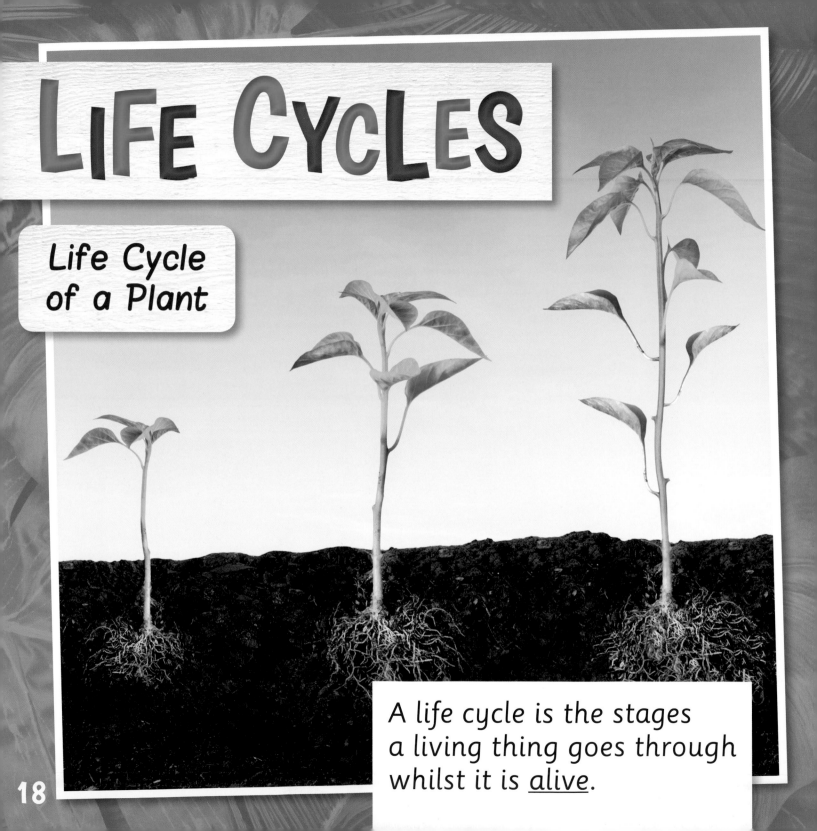

LIFE CYCLES

Life Cycle of a Plant

A life cycle is the stages a living thing goes through whilst it is <u>alive</u>.

Most plants start life as seeds. Roots grow from the seed to keep it <u>sturdy</u>.

PLANT SEEDS

The plant starts to grow a stem and a flower.

New seeds are growing inside the flower.

The new seed starts the cycle again!

When the time is right, the flower <u>releases</u> the new seeds, which land on the ground.

21

GROW YOUR OWN!

It's time to see plants grow in real life.

Watering plants is very important.

Buy some seeds at a <u>garden centre</u> and <u>sow</u> them in a pot by a window.

Now watch them grow!

GLOSSARY

absorb	take in or soak up
alive	living, not dead
garden centre	a shop that sells things for your garden, such as plants
releases	lets go of something
sow	to plant or scatter in the ground
sturdy	strong and stable

INDEX